———————————— ✦ ————————————

"(Our) struggle is a very beautiful thing...
the struggle that we go through as
human beings enables us to develop,
to take on further dimension."

—Jacob Lawrence

COME LOOK WITH ME

Discovering African American

Art for Children

James Haywood Rolling, Jr.

ini Charlesbridge

Published by Charlesbridge
85 Main Street
Watertown, MA 02472
(617) 926-0329
www.charlesbridge.com

Originally published by Lickle Publishing, Inc.

Library of Congress Control Number
2004115468

ISBN-13: 978-1-890674-07-6 (reinforced for library use)
ISBN-10: 1-890674-07-9 (reinforced for library use)

Series producer: Charles Davey
Text and picture selection by James Haywood Rolling, Jr.,
The School at Columbia University

Production & Design: Charles Davey *design* LLC
Printed and bound by C & C Offset Printing Co. Ltd.
in Shenzhen, Guangdong, China

(hc) 10 9 8 7 6 5 4 3

Contents

Preface

This book is filled with artwork that examines several key questions African Americans have struggled to address, perhaps more than any other people group in the United States. Who are we as a people? Who am I as a human being? What is my value to the world? African Americans have had to create a new identity as valuable citizens in a nation where the first African men, women and children were transported here to be treated as little more than beasts of burden.

Each and every African American is the descendant of people who were brought to this continent as slaves: people who were actively denied the equal rights and opportunities to better themselves that are promised to all citizens in the nation's founding documents; people who were belittled in literature, popular entertainment and visual culture as being less intelligent, less significant, and less blessed of the beauty that other cultures claimed. In the face of these painful barriers and the evils of racial discrimination, African Americans have made great contributions to the building of this nation. As one of those contributions, African Americans have created art that has made our beauty, our intelligence, our strength, and our humanity plainly visible for all to see. Our ability to overcome our peculiar hardships with grace and insight continues to be our unique contribution to contemporary civilization.

The artwork presented in this book is a small representation of a very remarkable effort by African Americans in the United States during the twentieth century to portray our developing self-image as citizens who have shaped not only ourselves, but have helped to develop the shape and color of all of our aspirations.

How to use this book

COME LOOK WITH ME: Discovering African American Art for Children is part of a series of art appreciation books for children. Like the previous books in the series, it may be shared with one child or a group of children. This book presents an interactive way of looking at art. Each of the twelve works of art is accompanied by a set of questions asked by the grade school children at The School at Columbia University, intended to stimulate thoughtful conversations between adults and children. There are no right or wrong answers to the questions.

The text that accompanies each full-page color plate includes background information on the artist and the work that can be read aloud by an adult or paraphrased to help guide children's conversations. It is best to limit each conversation to two or three works of art at a time in order to keep the interaction lively. When children are talking about the image, encourage them to point to specific parts of the image while they discuss it.

This book can be used at home, in the classroom, and in museums. When possible, it is always better to see the image in real life. The methods given here can help children learn a way of looking at original works of art and encourage them to share their understanding with others.

PALMER HAYDEN, *The Janitor who Paints.*
1937. Oil on canvas. 39½ × 32⅞".
Smithsonian American Art Museum, Washington, DC / Art Resource, NY.

Who are these people? What are they doing?

Is the man in a house? Why is there a garbage can next to him?

Why is the man painting?

Palmer Hayden (1890 – 1973) was born Peyton Cole Hedgeman in Widewater, Virginia. He was a World War I Army veteran who received the nickname Palmer Hayden when his commanding officers could not pronounce his given name. Hayden made important contributions to the depiction of African American folklore.

Folklore is comprised of traditional stories passed down in a community from generation to generation because the stories hold ideas important to that community. Hayden once created a series of twelve paintings on the subject of African American folk hero John Henry. Go and find a book about John Henry, and read the story of the great big steel-driving man who helped build the railroads of America. In the spirit of that hard work and those long hours, Palmer Hayden took ten years to complete his series of paintings.

Looking at Hayden's painting, *The Janitor Who Paints*, one encounters a scene in a cellar apartment in an unknown apartment building. The painter in the painting, his two subjects, the cat and all the other objects in the room are placed very close to one another to give a sense of how small the apartment is. In an interview, Hayden revealed that the painting is of a friend named Cloyd L. Boykin. Hayden explained the painting was a "protest painting." Nobody recognized Boykin as a talented artist, so he was forced to take a job as a janitor to put food on the table. While other people may have seen Boykin as only a janitor, Hayden was bold enough to recognize and to honor the desire to create works of lasting beauty in the heart of a man who was only expected to throw out trash. With this painting, Hayden called his friend a painter.

CLEMENTINE HUNTER. *Baptism.*
c. 1964. Oil on canvas. 15½ × 19½".
The Collection of David C. Driskell.

Why are people coming out of a church? Are those people nuns?

Why is the door of the building not as big as the people coming out of it?

Is one of the ducks sitting on a nest?

Is the other duck looking for food?

Clementine Hunter (c. 1887 – 1988) is one of the most celebrated American self-taught artists of the twentieth century. She did not begin painting until she was more than fifty years old and died at the age of 101. Hunter's artwork focused on the life shared by the community of rural African Americans who worked on the Melrose Plantation in Natchitoches, Louisiana not far from where she was born in Cloutierville. Melrose was a cotton plantation founded in the 1790's by a freed slave and her son. Hunter lived on the Melrose plantation for most of her life, first picking cotton as a farm hand, and later working in the plantation's main house as a cook and maid.

In 1898, Melrose was sold. The new owners liked to invite writers and painters to stay. Melrose became a famous artists' colony, that is, a gathering place for artists. One day Clementine Hunter asked permission to paint a picture. She painted an image of a baptism in the Cane River on a window shade. Fortunately the plantation's library curator saw her work and he encouraged her to do more.

Clementine Hunter is known as a folk artist. Folk artists paint in an untrained style that pays little attention to proper proportions or perspective in drawing. Folk art emphasizes strong patterns, simple colors and often looks like children's drawings and paintings.

Baptism is the depiction of a religious ceremony that Hunter would paint over and over again. A child is being held safely in the water by two church elders and is ceremonially cleansed and made new in a ritual of great importance to the African American church in the rural south. It is not hard to imagine Clementine Hunter, after spending most of her life as a simple laborer, felt born again into a new life as an artist and storyteller.

HENRY OSSAWA TANNER. *The Banjo Lesson.*
1893. Oil on canvas. 49 × 35½".
Hampton University Museum, Hampton, Virginia.

Is the old man trying to teach the boy a song?

What is that instrument they are holding in their hands?

Why are those pots on the floor?

Are they all alone in the house?

Henry O. Tanner (1859 – 1937) was born the son of a deeply religious family in Pittsburgh, Pennsylvania. On January 1, 1863, in the middle of the Civil War, and not long after Tanner was born, President Abraham Lincoln declared freedom for all remaining slaves. Lincoln's Emancipation Proclamation was a signal of important changes and new possibilities for the entire African American population of the United States.

Tanner's father was a bishop in the African Methodist Episcopal Church and wanted his son to follow him into the ministry. But when Tanner was 17, he went to see the 1876 Centennial Art Exhibit, held in the city of Philadelphia, where his father had been appointed minister of a new church. There he encountered the works of two African American artists—sculptor Edmonia Lewis and painter Edward Mitchell Bannister—and decided to become an artist as well. Although successful, Tanner found the rising racial intolerance in America too great. At 32, he went on a tour of Europe where he stopped in Paris, France, and decided to settle. He died there at 78, accepted and honored as a painter.

Tanner once said that the artist "who has the most sympathy with his subject will achieve the best results." The Banjo Lesson tells the story of a child honoring the wisdom and lessons freely offered by his elder. The subjects in the painting do not have many possessions, but they do have one another. The painting communicates the love and responsibility within the African American family. Tanner painted *The Banjo Lesson* to raise the self-image of African Americans, and to change our image in the eyes of those who brought so much harm to the African American community.

Tanner was also honoring his own father—who was not only a minister, but also a journal editor, and teacher. His father made positive statements from the preacher's pulpit; Tanner made his positive statements with a paintbrush.

CHARLES ALSTON. *Girl in a Red Dress.*
1934. Oil on canvas. 26 × 22".
The Harmon and Harriet Kelley Foundation for the Arts.

Who is this a painting of? How old is she?

Where is she? What is she looking at?

What might this girl be feeling?

Charles Alston (1907 – 1977) was born in Charlotte, North Carolina, the son of a highly respected Episcopal minister. Before Alston was three years old, his father died. Alston's mother remarried and the family moved to New York City, but Alston spent every summer in North Carolina until he was about 12 years old.

Alston was intrigued with the red clay of North Carolina. He would get buckets of it, put it through strainers and make things out of it—he once made the head of Abraham Lincoln! These were Alston's first art experiences. To him, "the whole creative thing is one of exploration of new or different ideas."

Alston studied art at Columbia University and New York University. He was an illustrator, graphic artist, sculptor, painter, and muralist. Alston was also an educator, teaching at places such as the Harlem Community Art Center and was appointed associate professor of painting at the City University of New York. He was a mentor to many other important African American artists such as Romare Bearden and Jacob Lawrence.

Girl in a Red Dress is vibrant with rich color, in contrast with the somber, serious expression on the young girl's face. We do not know who the girl is but she appears to have great confidence in herself. She sits in front of us tall and straight, head held high. Perhaps she is about to answer an important question, or perhaps she is about to ask one.

AARON DOUGLAS. *Boy with Toy Plane.*
1938. Oil on canvas. 22½ × 17".
The Walter O. Evans Collection of African American Art.

Is he sick?

Is he waiting for something?

What happens to a dream deferred? – Langston Hughes

Aaron Douglas (1898 – 1979) was born in Kansas, and received a degree in art from the University of Nebraska. He taught in Kansas City schools for a few years and then began to study with Winold Reiss, an illustrator from Germany who had a special interest in drawing the portraits of African Americans and Native Americans. Reiss encouraged Douglas to look to African art for inspiration in his work.

Douglas's use of African design and subject matter in his work brought him to the attention of some of the leading intellectuals of the 1920's Harlem Renaissance—also called the "New Negro Movement." Renaissance means re-birth: in the decades following Lincoln's 1863 Emancipation Proclamation, African Americans found new opportunities to educate themselves and improve the possibilities for their children to rise up and become much more than unskilled laborers

Douglas was proud to be African American. He once said, "let's bare our arms and plunge them deep through laughter, through pain, through sorrow, through hope, through disappointment, into the very depths of the souls of our people and drag forth material crude, rough, neglected. Then let's sing it, dance it, write it, paint it."

In *Boy with Toy Plane*, Douglas has painted a sensitive study of a boy on a stool with a toy plane in his hands. The boy's face seems to express disappointment, as if his toy plane no longer satisfies him. Douglas uses the face of the boy as a mirror to show the world that African Americans oppressed by racial segregation in America were capable of the same discontent all humans feel when things are not right with the world.

In 1940 Douglas moved to Nashville, Tennessee, where he founded the Art Department at Fisk University and taught there for 29 years before retiring.

SARAH ALBRITTON. *The Swimming Hole.*
1993-94. Acrylic on paper. 18 × 24". Private collection. Photo © Peter Jones, Courtesy Susan Roach,
Louisiana Regional Folklife Program, Louisiana Tech University.

How many children are swimming?

Is the water cold or warm?

Do they have anyplace else to play?

Sarah Albritton (1936 –) was born in Arcadia, in north central Louisiana. Her given name was Sarah Mae Drayton. At age twelve, Sarah was already earning her living, as the head cook at Tech Hitching Post Restaurant. During times of strict segregation in the United States, Sarah held many cooking jobs, often at the same time. In her early adult years she developed private businesses doing catering and home canning, in addition to farming, working as a housemother, the operator of a janitorial service, and a store manager.

Starting in 1993, about three years before her sixtieth birthday, Sarah picked up a paintbrush and some acrylic paints and began a series of self-taught paintings and stories of her personal experience. As Clementine Hunter was, she is a true folk artist.

Albritton is a storyteller and uses her paintings to tell us her story, to take a new look at herself with all of her bumps and bruises. In her images she always tells the truth about the struggles and the triumphs in her life.

Of her painting, *The Swimming Hole*, Albritton writes "it was a cesspool branch, but it was our swimming hole." Albritton grew up in poverty so great that children swam in the runoff from a sewage treatment plant, but when you look at this painting what Sarah shows is that all children will find a way to have their day in the sun.

WILLIAM H. JOHNSON. *Children Playing London Bridge.*
c. 1942. Watercolor on paper. 12 × 10½".
The David C. Driskell Collection.

What are they doing? What type of dance is it?

Why are they all wearing light colors?

Why are some of them wearing high heels and different color socks

---

William Henry Johnson (1901 – 1970) was born in Florence, South Carolina. As a rural African American child he did not have access to training in the arts in school, so he taught himself to draw by copying cartoons. He moved to Harlem in 1918, and worked at manual labor and service jobs until deciding to become a cartoonist. In 1921 Johnson enrolled himself in the National Academy of Design. Within the next five years he went from drawing cartoons to more ambitious oil paintings. He left the United States for France in 1926 to study art in Europe, and to work and exhibit his paintings.

Johnson was very influenced by the European Expressionist artists. Expressionists used distorted lines, shapes and exaggerated colors to show emotion and the inner vision of the artist rather than painting the exact representation of nature. He returned to America in 1938, just before the start of World War II, using the new style of painting he had learned with its bright colors and simple forms with heavy outlines. Johnson once wrote: "my aim is to express in a natural way what I feel, what is in me, both rhythmically and spiritually, all that which in time has been saved up in my family of primitiveness and tradition, and which is now concentrated in me."

His relatively brief but brilliant career as a painter ended when his mental and physical condition deteriorated because of serious illness. In 1947, Johnson was admitted to a hospital in New York. He never again painted and died in the hospital in 1970.

Johnson's study of African sculpture contributed to the large hands and feet and the elongated heads of the people in his paintings. One can also see his memories of rural South Carolina in his depictions of African American everyday life. In *Children Playing London Bridge* Johnson laces together bodies and arms swirling at play and expresses his love for the pleasures of childhood.

HUGHIE LEE-SMITH. *Boy with Tire.*
1952. Oil on prestwood panel. 23 × 29". Gift of Dr. S. B. Milton, Dr. A. Owen. Dr. B. F. Seabrooks, and Dr. A. E. THomas, Jr.
Photograph © the Detroit Institute of Arts. © Estate of Hughie Lee-Smith / Licensed by VAGA, New York, NY.

How old is this boy? Where is he?

Is he homeless?

What is he feeling?

Where are the rest of the people?

Why is the boy carrying a tire next to him?

Hughie Lee-Smith (1915 – 2000) was born in Eustis, Florida. His parents separated and he moved with his mother to Cleveland, Ohio where he went to school. He graduated from the Cleveland School of Arts with high honors. Lee-Smith studied theater and dance along with the visual arts and his performing arts training is easy to see in his paintings, which often appear at first to be stage sets. Lee-Smith received many awards for his artwork. In 1984 the City of Cleveland declared a Hughie Lee-Smith Day.

Lee-Smith's paintings portray African American life as survival in the midst of senseless neglect. He is a realistic and yet magical painter and uses a surrealistic style of painting to explore his concern with the loneliness of urban life and its decay. Surrealism was a style of art in the early twentieth century that emphasized dream-like images and other bits and pieces. These pieces are placed together for reasons that can't entirely be explained except that they help create a mood or feeling that runs underneath surface appearances.

In the painting *Boy with Tire*, a young boy stands in a wasteland. The buildings around him are isolated and dying, with cracked walls and broken windows. In some inner city or rural African American neighborhoods, children have no playgrounds to play in and are too poor to own their own store-bought toys. But children are brilliant at inventing games to play. One game involves finding an old tire and rolling it alongside you as you run beside it pushing it with your hand or a stick. The goal is to keep the tire from wobbling and toppling over. The boy in this painting stands alone, but through the use of his imagination he can stand with a purpose that overcomes his loneliness.

ELIZABETH CATLETT. *Harriet.*
1975. Linocut on paper. 12¼ × 10".
© Elizabeth Catlett / Licensed by VAGA, New York, NY.

What is the woman pointing at?

Are they in danger?

Where is everyone going? Why are they outside at night?

Why is the woman bigger than all the other people?

Elizabeth Catlett (1915 –) is a printmaker and sculptor, the granddaughter of former slaves. In the early 1930s she was refused admission to Carnegie Institute of Technology because of racial discrimination, so Catlett enrolled at Howard University, Washington, D.C., where she studied painting and design under the teaching of African American artist Lois Mailou Jones, with the intent of becoming a textile designer. Catlett later changed her major to painting and graduated with honors in 1937.

Catlett was the first person to earn an M.F.A. degree from the University of Iowa, in 1940. One of her teachers, the well-known American Regionalist painter Grant Wood, encouraged his students to make art about the people, places and ideas they knew best and also to experiment with different art media. Catlett learned to create masterful lithographs, linoleum cuts, and sculptures in wood, stone, clay, and bronze, all based on the lives and struggles of people of color.

In 1946 Catlett went to Mexico to study the lives of Mexicans there. She joined the Taller de Gràfica Popular in Mexico City, a prominent group of printmakers, and worked collectively with the artists in developing the art of the socially relevant print. Catlett has had more than fifty solo shows of her work, and now continues to make art while dividing her time between New York City and Cuernavaca, Mexico.

In the black and white print titled *Harriet*, Elizabeth Catlett revisits her portrayal of the African American hero Harriet Tubman, whom she depicted in print three times between 1946 and 1975. Tubman was a leader in the Underground Railroad, risking her life many times to lead escaping slaves to freedom in the North. With the same spirit and courage as Harriet Tubman, Catlett's vision, to depict the struggles of poor and working people of all colors, makes her a leader in the visual arts.

JACOB LAWRENCE. *Brownstones.*
1958. Egg tempera on hardboard, 31½ × 37¼".
Courtesy of Collection of Clark Atlanta University Art Galleries.

Why is everyone outside? Are they all friends and family?

Is this a block party? Where do the doors lead to?

Why are some of the children barefooted?

Are the two girls who are jumping rope sisters?

Jacob Lawrence (1917 – 2000) is an important twentieth-century American painter, recognized for his well-researched historical narratives and scenes of urban life in the African American community. When he was only twenty-four years old, his exhibition of a series of sixty paintings entitled "The Migration of the Negro" won him national recognition. Lawrence wanted to tell the story of the African American experience accurately, with no distortions or parts left out, creating a new "social realism."

Lawrence's parents were Southern, and migrated North to seek a better life. Jacob was born in Atlantic City, New Jersey. He arrived in Harlem with his family as a young boy. Artist Charles Alston, then a boy's work director at a community house in Harlem, immediately noticed that the talent Jacob had was different from other children's. Jacob was usually quite definite about what he wanted to do and extremely focused on achieving it.

As a teenager, Lawrence made frequent visits to the Metropolitan Museum of Art. He developed an appreciation for the works of old masters and modern masters of painting. At the same time, Lawrence was exposed to many of the leading black intellectuals and artists of the Harlem Renaissance.

Lawrence created a unique and original style. He combined the tempera technique (color pigment mixed with egg yolk thinned with water) with careful and geometric compositions. No shape or space or color was unplanned.

Brownstones are a kind of apartment building found in New York made of a particular kind of stone; they line up next to each other in a row. In Lawrence's 1958 painting titled *Brownstones*, the energy of the people in the Harlem neighborhood shown here pours into the streets. The colors glow. The doors and windows to the buildings are wide open, as wide open as the possibilities for the children playing outside on the sidewalk.

ELLIS WILSON. *Funeral Procession.*
1940. Oil on composite board. 30½ × 29¼". Aaron Douglas Collection,
Amistad Research Center at Tulane University, New Orleans.

Where are these people going?

Is it a rainy day or a sunny day?

Are the people in the background in the same line as these people close by?

Why are they dressed up so special?

Ellis Wilson (1899 – 1977) is quoted as once explaining, "My project or plan doesn't take much telling. I want to paint!…There is so much to paint and so little time." Born in Mayfield, Kentucky, Wilson one of six children. His father was a barber by trade, but was also an amateur painter. Wilson acknowledged that his artistic talent came from his father. Unfortunately, his father had to give up painting to support his growing family and he did not live to see his son's achievements as a painter.

Ellis took odd jobs to help out with the struggling family's finances. Once, when he was still young and working as a janitor for a dress shop in his hometown, Wilson drew a portrait on the store's window in cleaning soap that attracted the attention of passersby, drawing them into the store. Seeing Wilson's talent was good for business, the storeowner encouraged weekly drawings.

Wilson wanted to study art, so at nineteen he left Kentucky and headed North to attend The School of the Art Institute of Chicago. As World War II ended, he traveled back through the South and down to the Caribbean island of Haiti, painting the descendents of slaves in everyday family and work settings. Wilson particularly enjoyed traveling in Haiti because of its tropical beauty, its music and dancing, and the fact that people of color were the ruling majority.

Funeral Procession is Wilson's best-known painting. As the somber funeral line winds its way up the tropical hill, the heat of the sun bears down on the people. The figures are black silhouettes with no facial features, their loose-fitted clothing revealing no folds or details. One figure holds an umbrella to block the sun's rays. The people are straight and proud and purposeful.

ROMARE BEARDEN. *Morning* .
1975. Collage on paper. 13½ × 17½".
© Romare Bearden Foundation / Licensed by VAGA, New York, NY.

What room is this? Why are the walls different colors?

Why is one person leaning over the other?

If you were standing in this room, what sounds do you think you would hear? What might you smell?

What would you see in the next room?

What might you see through the green, green window?

Romare Bearden (1911 – 1988) was a painter, printmaker, and collage artist. Born in Charlotte, North Carolina, his family joined the great migration of Southern African Americans who moved North seeking a better life and more opportunities. Bearden grew up in Harlem, where his mother became the New York editor of the Chicago Defender, a widely read African American weekly newspaper. He studied at New York University and the Art Students League in New York City and went on to produce more than 2,000 works of art.

Both Romare's parents, Bessye and Howard, were prominent in the Harlem community, and well-known African American artists, musicians and writers, such as jazz composer Duke Ellington and poet Langston Hughes, were frequent visitors to the Bearden home. Such visits helped foster in Bearden a lifelong interest in jazz and literature, which were often the subject of his artwork. Another source of inspiration for Bearden were his many visits with relatives in Mecklenburg County of North Carolina and in Pittsburgh.

Bearden's collages are complex and layered, full of geometry, color, and textures created from spray paints and inks, wallpaper, posters, fabrics, foils, and miscellaneous found materials. He used collage to express the accumulation of his memories of rural and urban African American life. Of these memories Bearden once said, "There are roads out of the secret places within us along which we all must move as we go to touch others."

Morning is a quiet scene of domestic African American life; perhaps it comes to us from one of Romare Bearden's secret places in his childhood memories. We are thankful he has shared this *Morning* with us.

--- ✧ ---

Go back and look through the paintings in this book.

Choose one artwork for today. How would you describe the people in this picture? Are they like you or different?

What things do you recognize in this painting? What things seem new to you?

What can you tell me about how this person lived? How did you arrive at that idea?

What questions would you ask the artist about this work, if s/he were here?

Pretend you are inside this painting…
What does it feel like to walk within the story it tells?

What do you think other people would say about this work? Why do you think that?

What do you think is worth remembering about this painting?

Return to this book another day and you may discover something new about these African American artists.

Keep looking!